Original title:
Wristbands and Shadows

Copyright © 2025 Creative Arts Management OÜ
All rights reserved.

Author: Zachary Prescott
ISBN HARDBACK: 978-1-80586-142-3
ISBN PAPERBACK: 978-1-80586-614-5

Tied to the Night

In a party of clowns, we all do sway,
With colors so bright, they take gloom away.
One tripped and fell, his laugh was a hoot,
His polka dot pants flew high like a chute.

Under a sky where the stars poke out,
A dance-off erupted, we all scream and shout.
Who knew that a twist could send our drinks flying,
While bubbles of laughter kept everyone trying.

Harmonies of the Past

A jingle of jests from yesterday's crew,
Each tale spun golden, like sunshine anew.
We giggled through mischief, our faces aglow,
Recalling the summer when nobody slow.

With tunes of the past, our feet can't sit still,
A conga line formed, oh what a thrill!
Then one tried to moonwalk, but slipped on a shoe,
And laughter erupted, 'Oh, what a view!'

Flickering Threads

In a web of colors, we swirl and we play,
Each wink that we share makes night feel like day.
A confetti of quirks, we toss to the breeze,
With every small tumble, we're dropped to our knees.

The giggles resound with tales that we weave,
Of moments we're sharing, so hard to believe.
With each little twirl and an accidental trip,
We toast with our drinks, never losing our grip.

Bonds in Darkness

When shadows come out for a late-night spree,
We dance in the dark, just wild as can be.
A whisper of chaos, a wink and a grin,
As we trip o'er toes, let the fun times begin!

In the twilight's embrace, we tumble and fall,
While laughter ignites, uniting us all.
A secret alliance of silliness shines,
With each goofy moment, our friendship aligns.

The Glow of Unseen Connections

In the dark, they shimmer bright,
Colorful links, a quirky sight.
Worn with pride, a jolly cheer,
They glow like fireflies, oh so near.

Twisted tales of friends they share,
Each one a story, a bond laid bare.
Wrapped around, they start to dance,
A laugh, a grin, a silly prance.

Threads of Memory

Tangled threads, oh what a mess,
Each a memory, a joyful guess.
Stitched with laughter, sewn with glee,
Patterns of fun, just wait and see.

Colors clash in wild delight,
A tapestry of silly nights.
Each loop a hug, a cheerful nod,
In this thread, even pranks are broad.

Echoes in Fabric

Fabric whispers tales of yore,
Every fold hides so much more.
Echoes giggle, dance, and play,
In every stitch, a bright bouquet.

They bounce and sway, a lively crew,
Memories painted in every hue.
A funky groove, a playful twist,
In fabric's fold, you can't resist.

Bands of Connection

Groups of colors, feel the glow,
Where friendships blossom, seeds we sow.
Each band a chuckle, a wink, a tease,
In playful moments, we take our ease.

Jumbled stories, all entwined,
In laughter's arms, a joy you'll find.
Connected tightly, a comical flow,
These silly loops, we wear, we show.

Fleeting Touches

In the park, we twirl around,
With silly moves that astound,
A slap on the back, a nudge of cheer,
Laughter echoes, loud and clear.

Our gang's a circus, wild and bright,
Silly faces, pure delight,
Juggling jokes like hot potato,
Rolling eyes, oh what a show!

Glimmers of Belonging

In a room bright with many hues,
We share secrets, and funny news,
Silly hats at a gathering spree,
Every grin feels like magic to me.

Dance like no one's watching, we say,
Trip over smiles in a playful way,
A wink, a giggle, friendships grow,
Together we shine, stealing the show!

Shape of Memories

Clumsy moves on the dance floor,
Stepping on toes, then laughing more,
The shape of our joy in every twist,
A scrapbook of moments that can't be missed.

Crafting stories with every bite,
Spilling drinks in a fit of light,
Wrapped in moments, a goofy hold,
These tales of fun will never grow old.

Tapestry of Time

Colorful threads weave and twist,
A clumsy dance we've all missed.
Patterns laugh and change their hue,
Tickling moments, old and new.

With each strand, a story grows,
Some are silent, some just flow.
Laughing fibers, weaving fate,
And in the chaos, we celebrate.

Old knits fraying at the seams,
Tangled tales and silly dreams.
As the yarn unravels, we find,
Wit and whimsy intertwined.

So, grab a loop and give a tug,
Knot your worries, give a hug.
In this fabric, we'll all blend,
With laughter that will never end.

Dynamic Shadows

Silly shapes dance on the ground,
Twisting and turning all around.
A giant hand waves like a clown,
While the sun laughs, never frowns.

The wall's a canvas, bright and free,
With playful figures, just like me.
A cat that prances, a dog that jumps,
Each shadow caught in giggle humps.

They stretch and shrink with a sway,
Chasing sunlight's fleeting play.
Every leap makes spirits soar,
As we trip over shadows galore.

So come and join this merry game,
Each twist and turn, no one to blame.
In this light-hearted masquerade,
We find joy that won't ever fade.

Veils of Meaning

Layers thick with laughter's thread,
Cloaks of secrets, lightly spread.
Each fold hides a quirky tale,
Beneath the smiles, we set sail.

Painted fabric, bright and bold,
Covers thoughts, both new and old.
A whisper hides in every seam,
Tickled by a giggling dream.

Unraveling, we tease the mind,
Funny truths we seek to find.
In the layers, we dive deep,
What we reveal makes laughter leap.

So, wear your veil, and dance about,
Kick up your heels, and sing out loud.
With every curtain drawn away,
We'll bask in joy, come what may.

Markers of Belonging

Little trinkets, fun to share,
Bold reminders, everywhere.
Doodles and charms, a vibrant mix,
Tales of joy in playful tricks.

We gather 'round with silly glee,
Every token tells a spree.
From mismatched socks to crazy hats,
Each one whispers, 'You're with me!'

These funny finds, they hold our ties,
Closer bonds beneath the skies.
In jumbled boxes, laughter swells,
Each knickknack echoes joyful bells.

So clasp your treasures, loud and proud,
Like badges worn above the crowd.
In the chaos, we find our song,
With markers that say, 'You belong!'

Echoes of the Soul

Bouncing bands around my wrist,
Like a dance that can't be missed.
They stretch and twist in silly ways,
A jester's laugh in a million rays.

Colors clash like socks gone wild,
An inner child, forever styled.
With every laugh that fills the air,
We forget the world, without a care.

Hopping here and bouncing there,
A rubber band, a simple dare.
They squeak like toys from days of yore,
In this parade who could ask for more?

In the glow of sunlit glee,
I find a band that loves to be.
Echoes ring like chimes on high,
A joyous shout, a silly sigh.

Circles of Time

Time spins round like a playful loop,
In a game of hopscotch, join the troupe.
Each step a bounce, a giggle shared,
As if life's plot is slightly impaired.

I wore them bright, like candy hues,
With every laugh, I'd change my shoes.
Twirl and swirl, in circles we go,
Like dizzy bees in a honey flow.

When moments stretch and then unwind,
We flip and flop, leave worries behind.
With every glance, we wink at fate,
In circles of joy, let's celebrate!

The clock laughs with every tick,
In a funhouse mirror, life's a trick.
Round and round let's spin and play,
In the circle of time, come what may!

Merging Paths

Two trails converge in a tangled mess,
Like mismatched socks, we must confess.
With laughter ringing, hearts collide,
On this wild ride, let's enjoy the slide.

Here comes a twist, oh what a sight,
A flip of fate, and all feels right.
We juggle dreams with goofy glee,
As paths entwine, so shall we be.

Along the way, we trip and laugh,
The road ahead, a wobbly path.
With every chuckle, the world will sway,
A fusion of fun in the light of day.

So take my hand, let's skip along,
In every turn, we'll find our song.
With laughter as our guiding star,
Together, we'll wander near and far.

Shadows of the Heart

In the twilight, giggles roam,
Casting silliness, we feel at home.
With shadows stretching, they do prance,
A dance of whimsy in every glance.

The night unveils its playful style,
As laughter echoes for a while.
We chase reflections in moonlit beams,
And spin our folly into dreams.

A shadow puppet shows delight,
With every giggle chasing the night.
In a world so vast, less serious, please,
Let's frolic and play with grace and ease.

So here we stand, hand in hand,
In the glow of laughter, so grand.
With hearts aglow, we choose to start,
A journey bright, shadows apart.

Ties to the Unseen

In the sun's glow, odd sights appear,
A stretching hand, a grin so near,
Colors tangled, a dance so bright,
Frogs start jumping, oh what a sight!

Invisible strings pull us tight,
Laughter echoes, day turns to night,
We're skipping stones, our shadows lead,
Chasing giggles—the wild and free!

Up on a whim, we play in the park,
Silly antics, igniting a spark,
A twist, a turn, we leap with flair,
Collecting moments, light as air!

Reality bends but smiles stay true,
Friendship shines in every hue,
With comical twists that make us sway,
In this wild game, who needs ballet?

Shades of the Heart

Beneath the canopy, we jest and jive,
The world spins fast, yet we feel alive,
With painted faces and cheese on a stick,
Our laughter spirals, oh what a trick!

We twirl in laughter, not a care in sight,
Silly sunglasses, everything feels right,
As we dodge the rain, we stomp in delight,
Our hearts are creaking, yet spirits are light!

A tickling breeze, a puddle-filled splash,
Jokes fly like kites, bouncy and brash,
We dance through the chaos, unbothered by fate,
Creating a rainbow, it's never too late!

So here in the quirk, we find our own art,
With smiles stitched tightly, we play the part,
In the tapestry woven with threads of cheer,
The shades of our joy keep us ever near.

Weaving Together Moments

Threads of laughter, colors collide,
Moments are stitched, side by side,
Each silly story, a patch on the roll,
We dive into fun, losing all control!

With every twist, the fabric unwinds,
Knots of adventure, joy interlined,
We spin in circles, our giggles a thread,
Tangled in mischief—the best kind of spread!

Fanciful tales, like ribbons unfurl,
Each slapstick move makes our heads whirl,
Glorious chaos in every event,
The fabric of friendship with time well spent!

So let's weave memories, both silly and bright,
Cupcakes and capers fill up our nights,
With each moment crafted, we cherish the scene,
The patterns of life are vibrant and keen!

The Legacy of Touch

A nudge, a poke, tickles that spark,
The joy we exchange ignites a mark,
High-fives and hugs that wiggle and sway,
With each gentle push, we brighten the day!

Our fingers so playful, they paint the air,
Creating a whirlwind with friendship to share,
In side-splitting schemes, our spirits take flight,
Drifting together, utopia feels right!

Slapstick moments, a clumsy ballet,
Stumbling together, we greet the new day,
In our touch lies the power, a quirk and a twist,
A legacy priceless—no chance to resist!

So let laughter echo, as memories bloom,
In the legacy built, there's always room,
For whimsical moments, banter, and cheer,
With touches of joy, we'll always be near!

Shaded Reminders

A colorful band upon my wrist,
Reminds me of the things I missed.
Laughing at the silly sights,
Dancing in the neon lights.

Bouncing like a rubber ball,
Goofing off, we heed the call.
With each twist and silly turn,
Unexpected joys we learn.

In a world where giggles reign,
We forget about the mundane,
Each flicker brings a joyful grin,
A race to see who'll lose their pin!

So let's embrace this playful vibe,
Wear our badges, take the ride.
Together in our merry mess,
What a funny little dress!

Clusters of Light

Bubbly laughs and silly flair,
Glowing friends fill up the air.
Wrist adornments, quirky styles,
We chase the sun for miles and miles.

Sipping soda, throwing cheer,
Catch the light, we have no fear.
Each twinkling band tells a tale,
Of epic wins and silly fails.

Ducks in rows like rubber charms,
Spinning 'round with open arms.
Connections bright, a joyful bunch,
Time flies fast, we laugh and munch.

So gather close, let's paint the night,
With colors bold and endless light.
In this funky, playful dance,
We grab our chance, and take a chance!

Facets of Togetherness

Jelly hues on every wrist,
Sticky fingers can't resist.
Silly faces, laughter's bell,
In this bubble, all is well.

We swap our charms, our wild ideas,
Catching giggles like butterflies,
The magic grows with every laugh,
A quirky, bright, collective path.

When we trip and fall in glee,
It's a dance, just you and me.
Juggling memories, full of cheer,
What a sight when friends are near!

So here's to us, the funny crew,
Bound by laughter, and a view.
With every twist and turn we make,
We cherish bonds that never break!

The Art of Presence

In a parade of colors bright,
We twirl and spin, hearts in flight.
Every moment's a little show,
With winks and jests that surely flow.

Instant selfies, duck faces too,
Capturing all we love to do.
Each snapshot's a snapshot delight,
Together we shine, oh what a sight!

With jangling sounds and silly songs,
We dance around where laughter belongs.
The art of fun, we boldly paint,
Life's a canvas, let's be quaint!

So as we laugh, let's freely roam,
Creating joy, we feel at home.
Our colorful lives, like sparkles spread,
Bring shimmer-filled moments as we tread!

Echoing Silhouettes

In a dance of light and glee,
They twist and turn, wild and free.
A band of colors, bright and bold,
Chasing laughter, stories told.

Bouncing here and bouncing there,
Making friends without a care.
Giggles hide behind each curve,
A playful twist, the joy we serve.

When shadows stretch, they tell a tale,
Of mischief, fun, and laughter's sail.
Together we leap, twirl, and sway,
In this joyous, whirling ballet.

So join the game, let's all unite,
In a world where heartbeats ignite.
With every color binding us tight,
We dance until the fall of night.

Patterns of Light and Dark

In a fabric woven with bright smiles,
We share a laugh that stretches miles.
Circles of joy, it seems, are here,
As patterns dance, they bring good cheer.

With every twist, a joke is spun,
Beneath the sun, we have our fun.
A subtle change when the moon glows,
In playful whispers, the laughter flows.

The silly antics come alive,
Where every giggle starts to thrive.
Tangles grow through thick and thin,
Reminding us how joy begins.

So let's embrace this game of chance,
With every step, we skip and prance.
In patterns bright, we're never stark,
As fun ignites the light and dark.

Threads of the Heart

A crafty stitch in vibrant hues,
Draws laughter out from tired blues.
With every thread that we entwine,
Our cheerful hearts begin to shine.

Silly knots and quirky waves,
Intra-weave all the fun we crave.
A tangle here, a twist right there,
Creating chaos, yet no despair.

With colors that jump and play around,
Tales of giggles and joy abound.
As time moves on, we hold it dear,
A tapestry of laughter near.

So grab a loop, let's spin and roll,
In this wild game that keeps us whole.
In threads that dance, we find our part,
In this delightful, silly art.

Interwoven Journeys

We wander paths of vivid schemes,
Together we chase the light of dreams.
In every step, a lesson gained,
As quirky fables keep us entertained.

A twist here, a flip there,
In this adventure, we have flair.
The road is dotted with bright delight,
As laughter fuels our spirit's flight.

With a bounce and a skip, we change our fate,
Every moment becomes our plate.
In winding streets and silly faces,
We weave our tales through all the places.

So let's embrace this merry ride,
With open hearts, and arms spread wide.
In every journey, fun ignites,
As we dance through days and starry nights.

Echoes of the Forgotten

In the attic, there's a hat,
Worn by a cat, imagine that!
It poops confetti, what a sight,
While dancing wildly through the night.

A rubber chicken on the floor,
It lets out squawks; oh, there's more!
The sock drawer sings its own tune,
As we all waltz with a broom.

Patterns in the Gloom

A polka dot tie, bright and bold,
Worn by Grandpa, 100 years old.
It twirls and spins, oh what a dream,
If only ties could laugh and scream!

Lost marbles roll under the bed,
One just whispered, "I'm not dead!"
A game of tag with dust bunnies,
Their fluffy tricks, oh how they're funny.

Ties to the Past

A vintage phone with a curly wire,
It rings with laughter, a rare desire.
Old photographs, they wink and grin,
At all the trouble we've been in!

Our socks mismatched, a fashion crime,
Yet strutting proudly, we're slicing time.
With tickled toes and glittery slips,
We dance through life, making quips.

Colors in the Dusk

A neon bird, it flaps and plays,
Painting the evening in silly ways.
With every flap, a giggle swells,
As it unveils its rainbow spells.

Twirly straws in a fizzy drink,
Make silly faces that truly blink.
With laughter echoing all around,
In twilight's glow, pure joy is found.

Luminescence in Twilight

In the dusk, they wiggle bright,
Little bands of sheer delight,
Fingers dance, they twist and twine,
Every color, so divine.

Laughter rings through winds so bold,
Silly tales and secrets told,
With each move, a spark ignites,
Creating joy in silly flights.

They slip and slide on wrists so free,
Like little fish in cheerful glee,
Chasing shadows, what a sight,
As colors clash in evening light.

Comfort in the Unknown

On this journey, we may roam,
Each twist feels just like home,
With every loop, a wacky cheer,
In the dark, laughter draws near.

Whispers catch on gentle breeze,
Funky styles with greatest ease,
Making friends, a wild array,
As we dance the night away.

Sharing stories, silly schemes,
Floating high on bubbly dreams,
No fears left to hold us tight,
As we giggle in the night.

Threads of Echoes

Faded whispers in the air,
Tiny loops without a care,
Every shade a tale to tell,
In this fun, we revel well.

Stretch and pull, the bands connect,
Wobbling laughs, what fun we've decked,
In the fray, we spin and dive,
In this moment, we feel alive.

Time unfurls like funky string,
Playful echoes laugh and sing,
Every spiral, twist, and loop,
Joins the party, starts to swoop.

Marked by the Past

Old colors fade, but joy remains,
Lost in memories like silly trains,
Each binding wraps a story true,
A tapestry of shades, a hue.

Links of laughter, years gone by,
With a chuckle, we wave goodbye,
To moments woven, warm and bright,
In shadows past, we find the light.

So here we stand, a wild crew,
With tangled threads, we waved at you,
On this journey, we'll keep the fun,
Under the glow of a setting sun.

Vows Woven in Yarn

Stitching laughter in a row,
Colors vibrant, smiles aglow.
Knots of friendship, tight yet free,
Wrapped around you and me.

Ticklish threads, a playful strain,
Looping round with silly gains.
Each twist a tale, a giggle bright,
In our loops, we find delight.

Wobbly stitches, artful mess,
A tapestry of happiness.
In every weave, a jest, a spark,
Creating joy from light to dark.

Tangled hopes in woolly schemes,
Crafting life from silly dreams.
Together, we spin a cheerful plot,
In every seam, laughter's caught.

Dancing with the Dark

Moonlight's hint on fleeting feet,
In the night, we find our beat.
Bouncing shadows, jiving low,
Whispers of fun in the flow.

Twirl around with giggles bright,
Hiding mischief in the night.
A moonlit jig, oh what a sight,
Merry echoes, pure delight!

Creeping forms play peek-a-boo,
Jumping high, as if on cue.
Laughter bursts through darkened air,
Dancing, spinning without a care.

In the silence, wisecracks thrive,
Creating joy, we feel alive.
Nighttime's jesters, we partake,
In shadows' waltz, smiles we make.

Emblems of Moment

Pinning laughter on the sleeve,
Memory badges we believe.
Silly symbols, chatty cheer,
We wear our hearts like souvenirs.

Each charm a quirk, a giggle shared,
Life's oddities, we are prepared.
Moments stitched with threads of glee,
Marking time so playfully.

Grinning trinkets dance along,
Jingling sweetly in our song.
Every badge a tale to tell,
In our laughter, we excel.

Memories shimmer, color bright,
Crafting joy from day to night.
Emblems of the fun we seek,
In every glance, giggles peak.

Intertwined Presences

A puzzle made of goofy faces,
Connected by our silly traces.
Strings of laughter, woven tight,
Together we embrace the light.

Frolicsome steps on this strange path,
Mixing giggles with the math.
Two hearts whisper, then collide,
In this dance, we'll never hide.

Entwined in jests, we bloom and grow,
Playing life like it's a show.
Every twirl, a new surprise,
In our fun, the true prize lies.

With each moment, our spirits rise,
Laughing freely beneath the skies.
Together forever, we decree,
In this chaos, we're meant to be.

Afterglow of Bonds

In the sun, we sport our ties,
Colors bright, they catch the eyes.
An unexpected twist of fate,
Who knew fun could feel so great?

Tangled up in silly games,
Laughing hard, forgetting names.
A dance-off on the grassy plain,
Our silly moves drive them insane!

When the night begins to chill,
We share stories, laughs, and thrills.
With every tale the laughter grows,
Creating bonds that lighten loads.

So here's to ties that bring us near,
A laugh, a hug, a gentle cheer.
With every twist, our joy expands,
These little things, like golden bands.

Charmed Connections

In a room so full of cheer,
We gather 'round, our crew is near.
With quirky hats and silly shoes,
We sport our charms, we cannot lose!

Each cross of arms, a playful sign,
With every joke, our smiles align.
An extra slice of cake for me?
It's friendship baked in harmony!

We raise a glass to new delight,
To laughter shared late in the night.
A game of 'who can dance the best?'
We stumble; laughter's our true test!

Tangled tales we weave with glee,
Every moment wild and free.
These bonds of joy make life a spree,
In charmed connections, we find glee.

Flickers of Memory

A camera click, the fun begins,
We capture every laugh and grin.
Moments bright, forever clear,
With friends like these, there's naught to fear.

Ponytails and hats askew,
Every mishap feels brand new.
We mime the moves of cartoon stars,
And wonder how we'll look from Mars!

We scribble notes on napkins small,
Inside jokes and memories tall.
A treasure chest of silly scenes,
In laughter's glow, we find our means.

So here's to days that shimmer bright,
When every banter feels just right.
With every flicker, time stands still,
In the laughter, we find our thrill.

Fabric of Dreams

In a patchwork quilt of giggles wide,
We sew our tales with silly pride.
Each thread a laugh, each knot a joke,
A tapestry where friendships poke!

Under stars, we weave a scheme,
With moonlit dances, we chase a dream.
Every twist and every turn,
In this fabric, we brightly burn!

With whispering winds and playful sighs,
We launch our hopes up to the skies.
A glitter bomb of sheer delight,
With every shimmer, our hearts ignite!

So gather round this woven scene,
Embrace the joy, let laughter gleam.
In this fabric, bound so tight,
We craft our dreams, bathed in light.

Secrets in the Fabric

In a world of patterns bright,
Where colors twist and turn,
Each stitch a little secret,
Of tales we long to learn.

A leopard and a polka dot,
Sipped tea beneath the sun,
Their friendship stitched together,
With laughter, oh so fun!

The stripes would tell a story,
Of mishaps and of cheer,
While paisleys danced in circles,
Igniting silly fear.

In the fabric of our dreams,
A world of joy is spun,
With every thread a giggle,
And every knot a pun.

Shades of Connection

Two colors met one rainy day,
And laughed beneath the gloom,
They held hands in a silly way,
Creating quite the room.

A hue of blue and lime,
Said, "Let's start a band!"
They strummed on stringy fortunes,
And danced upon the sand.

The shades would sway and giggle,
In the sunlight's warm embrace,
While every line and angle,
Shared a silly face.

With every twist and turn they tak,
Their bond began to grow,
In the art of goofy layers,
The brightest hues aglow.

The Dance of Time

Tick-tock went the rubber band,
As seconds slipped away,
It bounced and twisted through the air,
In a polka dot ballet.

The clock wore goofy socks,
And tripped upon the floor,
As moments danced in cha-cha leaps,
With giggles evermore.

Each hour a comedian's act,
Time played a funny game,
With every tick a laughing jest,
And every tock the same.

The rhythm of our laughter,
Echoed through the years,
In the dance of quirky moments,
We twirled with joyful cheers.

Binding Colors

Two shades bound tightly, side by side,
They tied a knot of fun,
A vibrant link of giggles bright,
Their journey just begun.

With every twist, a tale to tell,
In colors bold and true,
The red and green, they knew so well,
That laughter grew and grew.

They painted rainbows in the sky,
Using smiles as their brush,
In a canvas filled with antics,
Creating quite the hush.

And as the day went drifting by,
Their bond became a theme,
In every hue and color,
They found their silly dream.

Shadows Wear Our Stories

In the corner of the room, they dance,
Twirling tales of whimsy and chance,
A mischief-maker in silly attire,
Each giggle a laugh, each step a fire.

Once lost in corners, now bold and bright,
They steal the sunshine, banish the night,
With every twist, they pull us near,
In their funny capes, there's nothing to fear.

Puppets of dusk, on a playful spree,
They make the mundane feel wild and free,
With sprightly steps and winks in their eyes,
They spin our tales like cartoon skies.

Glimpses of life through a jester's lens,
Finding the joy that never ends,
In a world where everything's upside down,
Laughter's the king, and we wear the crown.

Tattered Dreams and Luminous Night

In pockets of laughter, dreams swirl and flit,
With frayed edges ticking, they never quite sit,
They shimmer and shine in the neon glow,
As the stars overhead giggle, sway, and bow.

Once lost and tangled, they twist like a vine,
Hitching a ride on a comet's spine,
In the fabric of night, they stretch and they weave,
With pixie dust whispers, they never deceive.

A whimsical circus beneath a pale moon,
Where echoes erupt and balloons go boom,
A tapestry woven from giggles and snorts,
We share in the joy that life sometimes courts.

Each tattered thread is a memory spun,
Worn by the playful, who bask in the fun,
So let's twirl through the night, with spirits so light,
In this tapestry of dreams, we welcome delight.

Bound by Fabric and Fate

Threaded together in a wild charade,
We dance like marionettes, unafraid,
Our fortunes entwined in a laugh and a grin,
With seams that embrace where the fun can begin.

In patterns eccentric, we waltz around,
With echoes of laughter like bugs in surround,
Each knot tells a story, each loop a tale,
A fabric of fables that never turns stale.

With patches of joy and swatches of cheer,
We stitch up the moments that make us all peer,
Into the kaleidoscope of glee, tight-laced,
In this playful symphony, we joyously race.

Banished are worries, with each playful thread,
Painting the world where mere mischief is bred,
So come—let's gather, with giggles, we'll weave,
A cozy cocoon, in which all can believe.

Underneath the Veil

Behind a curtain, we hide and we dart,
Playing our tunes, a merry old art,
With chuckles and snickers, we plot and we play,
In this silly masquerade, come join in the fray.

With masks made of memories and laughter we share,
We craft a ruckus without any care,
Each flap of the fabric tells secrets so bold,
Bringing warmth to the tales that never grow old.

Underneath the veil, we tumble and roll,
We're jesters at heart with a jubilant soul,
Sharing our quirks with a wink and a jig,
In the grand tapestry, our laughter's the gig.

So lift the curtain, let the shenanigans reign,
In this whimsical world, we'll never feel pain,
With joy as our guide and fate in our hands,
We'll dance through the night in our comical bands.

Fabric of Our Echoes

In a whimsy shop, we trade our cheer,
Bright colors clash, but we hold them dear.
Laughter echoes, sparking delight,
As we twist and twirl into the night.

Each thread tells stories from times so bold,
Of goofy dances and secrets told.
We weave our joy with every strand,
In this zany world, we take our stand.

Balloons tied high, we float with glee,
A knot of friendship, you and me.
As we prance and sing, our voices blend,
This fabric of laughter will never end.

So come, my friend, let's join the spree,
With every strand, we make history.
In the weave of fun and silly schemes,
We stitch our fate with laughter's beams.

Ethereal Ties

Two goofy souls with a twisty plan,
Tie silly knots, as only we can.
With hairdos wild, we strut around,
Remarkable ties, where fun is found.

Our bonds are light, like feathers they float,
In a sea of giggles, we happily gloat.
As whimsical colors dance in the air,
With each funny story, we showcase flair.

Our antics spark joy, oh what a sight,
Like chasing rainbows, from morning to night.
We weave our tales on a tapestry bright,
Ethereal ties, a humor-filled flight.

So let's unleash laughter, come take a ride,
Through giggle-filled realms, side by side.
In this world of fun, we'll proudly steer,
Bound by our laughter, nothing to fear.

The Weight of Light

In a world where giggles float like air,
We wear our smiles, without a care.
Each chuckle's a feather, oh what a sight,
We dance through the day, it feels so right.

With each silly joke that we declare,
The weight of our laughter lightens the air.
In every moment, we find a tease,
Creating memories with perfect ease.

Like marshmallow clouds, our laughter flies,
Bouncing off walls, in a grand surprise.
With bubbles of joy that pop and gleam,
Life feels like a hilarious dream.

So gather around, and let's celebrate,
With humor and fun, we'll elevate.
For joy is light, and laughter is key,
In this jolly dance, forever we'll be.

Faded Threads and Flickering Lights

In the attic where old memories rest,
Lurk faded threads, a quirky jest.
With flickering lights above our heads,
We spin tales of socks and silly spreads.

Each laugh is a thread, some worn and frayed,
Stitching our hearts in a humorous parade.
With twinkling eyes and wild grins,
We reminisce where the laughter begins.

Around the corner, a prank awaits,
With echoes of chuckles from funny traits.
Our friendship's woven in a patchwork quilt,
Crafted with giggles and laughter built.

So come now, dear friend, let's spin our yarns,
In this zany world, there're no alarms.
With faded threads and lights that play,
Let's capture joy in a splendid display.

Chasing the Gloom

In a world where colors clash,
Bright bands laugh and play,
Stripes and dots all in a dash,
They keep the dullness at bay.

Glimmering hues dance in the breeze,
Whispers of joy in each sway,
Chasing away the old unease,
A party that's here to stay.

With giggles and twirls, we delight,
Bright smiles worn like a crown,
Each twist spins shadows so light,
Life's worries kept upside down.

So we leap over puddles of gray,
Each step is a bounce, a cheer,
Forgetfulness in vibrant display,
No gloomy thoughts will come near.

Remnants of Touch

In the laughter of a silly dance,
They jingle and jive with flair,
Remnants of past mischief's chance,
Tangled in memory, we share.

Faded ties from days gone by,
Always bring a chuckle or two,
Each thread holds a story nearby,
In knots of joy, we grew.

Bouncing back with every move,
They guide us through old ruckus,
In their embrace, we find our groove,
Like playful shadows with gusto.

So let's revel in the glee,
Unravel stories bound tight,
With remnants reminding me,
That laughter is our best light.

Guardians of the Past

With colors bright and laughter loud,
They guard secrets in playful clinks,
A loyal crew, a vibrant shroud,
They hold the moments, or so it thinks.

Swirling tales of clumsy fate,
Adventures we may (or may not) recall,
Each hue shaped a joyful trait,
In a bundle, we stand tall.

Worn down by time yet still alive,
They poke fun at what we've done,
In whimsical ways, they thrive,
Our laughter echoes just for fun.

Forever tied, we dance anew,
Twisting tales in every spin,
Guardians of life's colorful crew,
Adventures waiting to begin.

Shadows of Sentiment

Underneath the laughing sun,
Two tones sprawl and tease,
Whispers of a life well run,
Dance lightly on the breeze.

They echo giggles from afar,
Casting shade with every glow,
With mischief like a shining star,
Their antics steal the show.

In moments lost, they find their way,
Draped in threads of silly chance,
They keep the dreary shades at bay,
And lead us in a comical dance.

We twirl through time, no need to fret,
These shadows, our fun-filled friends,
With bright colors we won't forget,
Life's laughter, it never ends.

Silhouettes of Emotion

In the corner, a goofy stance,
A dance moves without a chance.
Laughter echoes, a silly sound,
Joy and folly twirl around.

Eager arms reach for the sky,
As dreams float by, oh so spry.
Chasing giggles, we slip and slide,
Our shadows copy, full of pride.

Underneath the twinkling lights,
A parade of clumsy sights.
We embrace each laugh and trip,
With every tumble, our spirits zip.

In this dance of whirling joys,
Wobbling like mischievous toys.
Through the night we won't slow down,
Creating giggles, wearing joy's crown.

Ties that Bind

A knot of friends, we play the game,
With silly faces, never the same.
Each twist and turn brings a new laugh,
In joy's equation, we're the math.

Wrapped up in a tale or two,
We spin our stories, all askew.
With play-dough minds and giggly sighs,
Our bonds grow stronger, reaching the skies.

One jumps high, the other falls,
In this chaos, friendship calls.
Together we're a wobbly bunch,
Finding joy in every punch.

So as we tie our jolly string,
Laughter's the tune that we all bring.
With bonds of fun that never snap,
We roam the nights, a merry map.

Specters in the Light

Figures shift in splashes bright,
The wobbly ghosts show off their height.
Waving arms and silly grins,
We dance through life, and laughter wins.

Peeking out from every nook,
Strange shadows play like storybooks.
In this fun house of the uh-oh,
Silly ghosts put on a show.

Quirky echoes bounce and sway,
Chasing giggles to lighten the way.
With every twirl, we find delight,
Our spectral dance runs wild and bright.

Through spirited nights, we skip and gleam,
In a funny world, we make the dream.
Where laughter hides in the soft glow,
In this spectacle, joy's in tow.

Colors of Remembrance

In hues of humor, we paint the scene,
Bouncing colors, a lively sheen.
Every shade tells a funny tale,
In memory's frame, let laughter sail.

Splashes of green for goofy quirks,
A bit of red for silly smirks.
Each moment captured, a vivid spark,
With dashes of joy lighting the dark.

Golden yellows wrap us tight,
In twirling dances, pure delight.
With every pop, we cheer and shout,
In this rainbow, we leap about.

So when the sun begins to fade,
We gather colors, no plans to trade.
In laughter's arms, we reminisce,
Embracing shades of joyous bliss.

Chasing Shadows of the Heart

In a park where giggles blend,
A raccoon steals all he can bend.
With underpants on his small head,
We chase him down, laughter spread.

A duck with dance moves like a star,
Waddles near, and we all roar,
He marches like he's in parade,
Twisting 'round, a frolic made.

A frisbee flies, a wild swoop,
It lands in soup—one giant loop!
Mama laughs, "You'll pay for that!"
As dad slips on the dog, how flat!

But in this sunny, silly spree,
The bonds we form—oh, can't you see?
No treasure chest could match this fun,
With every laugh, we're all as one.

Layers of Light

The sun, it twinkles, plays a game,
While shadows dance without a name.
The cat springs high, a leap of fate,
As coffee spills—what an estate!

In puddles deep, reflections bloom,
Each one a giggle, conjures room.
Jump through the mirror, feet a splash,
Oh look, it's me, with glasses—smash!

The breeze carries balloons away,
A loop-de-loop, a jester's play.
We chase them high, our voices blend,
In this bright show, around the bend.

At twilight's hour, fired up delight,
We share our tales, oh what a sight!
These layers of joy, let them ignite,
With laughter echoing through the night.

Boundless Reflections

Two friends in hats, a goofy duo,
One spins tales, the other, 'Whoo-hoo!'
With mirrors held to show their flair,
They stick their tongues out, unaware.

A puddle forms right by our feet,
"Jump in!" one shouts, "It'll be a treat!"
A splashy surprise, a watery fight,
Endless giggles through the night.

The moon peeks down, a smirk in light,
As we crown squirrels, a regal sight.
Acorns tossed, who gets the gold?
A prize of snacks, if stories told.

Each silly moment, a ribbon tied,
In this fun race where joys collide.
Boundless echoes, memories bright,
In reflections shared, we take flight.

Threads Woven in Silence

A hoodie here, a cloak of fun,
Stitched with secrets, one by one.
We play hide and seek with puns,
And silly faces, little runs.

With twinkling lights on penguin hats,
We waddle 'round like silly chats.
A yarn so bright, a colors' whirl,
Tangled threads, a laughter swirl.

A paper crane takes flight with grace,
But lands a funny spot—my face!
A chuckle breaks the quiet air,
As friends unite without a care.

In this woven world, we find our cheer,
With whispers loud and hearts sincere.
Threads of humor color our days,
In joyous knots, we weave our play.

Whispering Fabrics

Colorful strips, a quirky twist,
They dance around like they just can't resist.
Worn on a wrist, they wiggle with glee,
Telling secrets, oh so carefree.

Some clash like cats, some flow like a stream,
They argue and laugh, oh what a team!
One's on a mission, the other's so bold,
With fabricy jokes that never get old.

A festival of flair, a carnival of cheer,
They tickle the skin, bring warmth to the near.
Stitched with bright laughter, they never get shy,
Leaving smiles behind as they flutter on by.

Silhouettes of Sentiment

In the glow of dusk, they prance and play,
Casting giggles and laughs on a bright sunny day.
Drapes of delight tease the light on the run,
Whispering tales of silliness, oh what fun!

Frolicking figures with a wink and a nod,
Every twist and turn, a whimsical prod.
They float in the breeze, a comical crew,
Carrying stories in each playful hue.

Like puppies in costumes, a jovial sight,
They're dressed to impress for this fabulously bright.
With nods and ha-has, they revel and play,
In the glow of the setting, they steal hearts away.

Glimmers Beneath the Surface

Beneath the bright fabrics, a tale unfolds,
Of sparkles and giggles, a sight to behold.
They shimmer in rhythms, a mischievous flick,
In the pools of laughter, they play their quick trick.

Jokes intertwined in the fibers they weave,
Hiding in hues that make one believe.
A twist and a turn, they spring to life,
Slicing through silence with comedic strife.

Each shade holds a chuckle, a snicker, a smile,
Bright colors of joy that stretch for a mile.
As sunlight spills secrets, they shimmer and brag,
Creating a tapestry of funny and fab.

Embraced by the Void

In corners of darkness, where laughter is shy,
A chance meeting happens, oh my, oh my!
They flutter like whispers through night's cozy shroud,
Turning frowns into giggles, oh aren't they proud?

With a squeeze and a stretch, they liven the gloom,
Casting bright spells that dispel all the doom.
Wrapped in odd fabrics that twist with delight,
They twirl in the moonlight, a real funny sight.

Jester-like, they tumble, they joke and they tease,
Filling the void with a fluttering breeze.
So here's to the mischief, the giggles we share,
In the cloak of the night, let's dance without care.

Threads of Memory

In a closet lost, all they sway,
A mishmash of colors, bright and gay.
They twist and tangle with glee at night,
Whispering secrets in the pale moonlight.

Each one a story, twisted in time,
Some are jazzy, some are sublime.
They dance on my wrist, a jolly parade,
While I chuckle at how they evade!

A blue one claims it holds my good luck,
The red one insists it knows how to pluck.
With each silly story, they make me laugh,
Turning my frown into a joyful gaff!

So here's to the loops of my funny old past,
They wrap around memories that seem to last.
With a wink and a nod, I wear them with pride,
As the colors of laughter become my guide.

Echoes in the Twilight

As twilight creeps, the hues get bold,
My charming collection, a sight to behold.
They shimmer and clink like a merry band,
Creating a symphony that's simply grand.

A tiny green one claims it's from Mars,
While the yellow insists it's kissed by stars.
Together they giggle, they sway side to side,
A troupe of misfits full of joy and pride.

They jostle and jiggle, with each little bump,
Reminding me daily that life's quite a jump.
With each heartfelt laugh, they weave a new thread,
And whisper sweet nothings as I lay in bed.

So here's to their magic, enchanting and wild,
A parade of colors that dance and are styled.
Their playful caress brings a grin to my face,
As memories shimmer, each giggle a trace.

Bands of Light and Dark

A rainbow of loops draped on the floor,
They're tussling and wriggling, what a colorful chore.
The black one jokes it's a ninja at night,
While the pink one just giggles, all airy and light.

Together they joke about life's little woes,
Guiding me on where the laughter flows.
Each band tells a tale, a fit of delight,
As they twirl in the twilight, oh what a sight!

They wrap around limbs like a confetti spree,
Unraveling humor where none used to be.
With one little tug, they tumble and roll,
Binding laughter tightly, uniting the whole.

So here's to the bands that prance through my days,
Crafting joy out of chaos, in whimsical ways.
In the dance of the evening, they flourish and play,
Ensuring my heart has a chuckle each day.

The Ties That Bind

With loops and curls flinging all around,
Each twist tells a joke, in laughter I'm bound.
The blue one insists it's got the best moves,
While the orange one's certain it grooves and proves.

They cheerfully jingle when I take a stride,
Making life merrier, never a divide.
From goofy to grand, they each have a role,
Crafting a tapestry that brightens my soul.

The one says it's magic, a ticket to cheer,
While another claims it's a wand, let's be clear.
They weave through my fingers, a circus of love,
And giggle as one takes a funny shove.

So here's to the ties that bind joy and jest,
In a carnival whirl, they're simply the best.
With every sweet memory, they hold on tight,
Creating a canvas that sparkles with light.

Nuances of the Night

Under the moon, we twist and twirl,
Strapped on colors, giving it a whirl.
Glows and giggles fill the delightful air,
As glow-in-the-dark creatures roam without a care.

Dancing in circles, with laughter so loud,
A mishap occurs, I trip on a cloud.
Falling like confetti, a sight so absurd,
As friends burst with laughter, life's sweetest word.

Each band a story, each tale a jest,
We wear our fabric, it's truly the best.
From moments at dusk to times of delight,
We gather our quirks, embracing the night.

Jingles and jests, a joyous parade,
Making memories that never will fade.
At dawn we shall chuckle, shaken but sound,
In the tapestry woven, true fun will be found.

Shadows Beneath the Surface

Hitch a ride on a comet, oh what a scene,
With matches and mayhem, we're all feeling keen.
Like bubbles that pop, we collapse with a cheer,
Chasing the giggles as the night draws near.

With echoes of laughter, we leap in the dark,
Our antics ignite like a wild, silly spark.
Invisible threads bind our banter and smiles,
While the moon plays the joker, juggling our wiles.

A slip and a slide, we dance with such flair,
The ground sneaks a chuckle, adding some air.
With shadows a-dancing, our spirits take flight,
In this grand adventure, everything feels right.

Through whispers and giggles, the night softly gleams,
Where friendships in chaos create the best dreams.
We build on the laughter, a world we embrace,
As whimsy and folly finds a cozy place.

Tellers of Tales

Gather around, dear friends, take a seat,
With fabric and flair, a whimsical treat.
Each story a riddle, wrapped round our wrists,
We dive into giggles, igniting our lists.

From pirates to dragons, we share our grand fate,
While wearing our tales, let's not hesitate.
With every strange twist, and laughter galore,
We unlock new adventures, opening doors.

The moon is the audience, oh what a show,
As we spin our wild tales, voices in tow.
With every new chapter, we stumble and soar,
Creating our legend, who could ask for more?

In this band of misfits, a treasure we find,
With laughter our language, we're of one mind.
Together we frolic, in merriment's glee,
As we tell our stories, forever carefree.

The Weight of Memories

Trinkets of laughter wrapped round our wrists,
Each moment we'll cherish, a friendship that exists.
With jokes that we share, and pranks that we pull,
Life's merry adventures, oh, aren't they a full?

We sashay through the night, like stars gone astray,
With colors and giggles, we brighten the way.
From silly mischiefs to secrets we keep,
In the dance of good times, our hearts take a leap.

The weight of our laughter, a treasure to hold,
With tales bursting forth, each memory bold.
In the tapestry woven, with threads of delight,
We'll embrace every moment, as we conquer the night.

So raise up a cheer for the moments we share,
For the weight of our laughter ignites everywhere.
In friendships, the fabric, we sew with our dreams,
Together we sparkle, or so it just seems.

Whispers of the Past

A rubber band snapped, oh what a sound,
Once a hero, now he's face down.
With laughter that echoes, we roamed the park,
Chasing memories that lit up the dark.

Old tales resurfaced, a trip down time,
Like socks in the wash, not quite in their prime.
We painted our faces with colors so bright,
Every mishap turned laughter's delight.

In the corner, a dance, a flail on the floor,
Attempting the moonwalk, we fell with a roar.
The past in our grasp, like candy so sweet,
Who knew that nostalgia could dance to this beat?

With giggles and jests, we bantered till noon,
Where the echoes of laughter sang out like a tune.
Time may have passed, but we remain bold,
With secrets embroidered in stories retold.

Lattice of Innocence

In a world made of bubbles, we floated away,
Chasing the sun on a bright sunny day.
With laughter like sprinkles on ice cream so sweet,
Each tumble and trip just added more heat.

We built up our castles with sand and with glee,
Until waves came to swallow them back to the sea.
A race with the seagulls, oh what a sight,
As we danced on the shore, full of pure delight.

With pockets of treasures, we'd barter and trade,
A crust of old bread for a game we had played.
In a lattice of dreams, so fancy and bright,
Innocence giggled, making wrongs turn to right.

When the clock strikes the hour, we'd vanish like smoke,
Yet each silly laugh was a promise, unbroke.
Though time may unfold, and we drift far apart,
We carry the echoes deep down in our heart.

The Unseen Embrace

In the middle of chaos, we found a new game,
Invisible ties, it never felt the same.
With a flick of the wrist, we conjured delight,
Connecting our laughter, as day turned to night.

A wink and a nod, we sketched in thin air,
The spirits of friendship twinkled, so rare.
Caught in a whirlwind of joy and of fun,
Each moment we shared was a race we had run.

In corners of silence, we spun round and round,
Where giggles would echo in whispers, profound.
To dance in unseen webs that we wove with our glee,
We floated like dreams, wild and fancy-free.

As the stars gave a wink, our secrets took flight,
And every embrace felt like magic, so light.
Though you couldn't quite see us, you felt the embrace,
A shimmer of joy that time couldn't erase.

Muffled Sounds of Union

Underneath a blanket of giggles and jest,
Our voices blended, each joke a small quest.
With whispers that danced like leaves on the breeze,
Unruly and free, just like silly tease.

We saw through the walls of faraway dreams,
Each muffled connection bursting at seams.
Like a pop of a balloon, bright laughter would rise,
Creating a friendship wrapped up in surprise.

In cozy old corners, we'd share every tale,
Like cats on a windowsill, snuggled and frail.
Through hiccups and snorts, we united as one,
Crafting our stories beneath the warm sun.

With free-spirited hearts, our laughter ran free,
A union of joy, overflowing with glee.
So here's to the echoes, the warmth and the cheer,
In muffled sounds woven, ever so dear.

Hues of Reflection

In colors bright, we dance and play,
Our laughter lightens up the day.
With every twist, we weave a tale,
Each vibrant hue lifts every veil.

Beneath the sun, we skip and spin,
With broad grins plastered on our skin.
A rainbow brought by joy divine,
Each sparkle shared, a perfect sign.

The tickle of a sun-kissed breeze,
Turns every frown to joyful tease.
In silly shapes, our stories blend,
In this mad world, we joyfully mend.

Let colors flash in bold delight,
A canvas bright, a pure delight.
With every laugh, our spirits soar,
In hues of joy, we want for more.

Fading Imprints

A jolly march along the sand,
With footprints wild that fate had planned.
Each little mark a giggle's trace,
As waves come in to steal our space.

We race and tumble, trip and slide,
In giddy circles, we confide.
The ocean roars, our names erased,
But echoes of our laughs are placed.

A silly hat, a flower crown,
All tossed around like merry clowns.
In playful nudges and friendly jest,
These fleeting moments are the best.

Though imprints fade like morning dew,
Our hearts will keep this colorful crew.
With every wave, we start anew,
In laughter's wake, that's how we flew.

Symbols of Solace

A quirky charm upon my wrist,
In silly stores, I can't resist.
With each bauble, a secret kept,
In jest we laugh, in fun, we leapt.

A doodle here, a smirk over there,
As stories spin through the night air.
While echoing joy with every thread,
Our precious quirks are warmly fed.

They shine like stars on a moonlit spree,
A mismatched pair, just you and me.
With every wink, we toast a cheer,
These charms remind us, laughter's near.

In silly symbols, we find our grace,
With playful hearts, we share our space.
Through every giggle, every glance,
In happiness, we'll always dance.

Whispering Threads

In tangled yarn of dreams we weave,
With threads of joy that never leave.
Each playful knot, a bond that's tight,
In silly stories, our hearts take flight.

As laughter flows like rivers wide,
Through elastic bands, our spirits glide.
A twist, a turn, a game we play,
In cheer and charm, we find our way.

Every stitch is a tale retold,
In goofy strides, our lives unfold.
With yarn so bright and eyes ablaze,
We stitch together our whirly days.

So let the whispers guide our thread,
With giggles sheltered in our head.
In colorful strands, we find our cheer,
In every twirl, we hold you near.

Silken Ties

In a world of threads so bright,
Chasing colors in the light.
Dancing patterns, swirling round,
Laughter echoes, joy is found.

Funky knots and funky bands,
Fingers fold like they have plans.
Twisting stories, tales of yore,
Who knew life could be such a chore?

Tickled pink, a duck quacks loud,
Threads unite the quirky crowd.
With every tug, a giggle bursts,
In this fabric, fun immerses.

Floating vibes on silly swings,
Tying dreams with rubber strings.
Oh the fun of getting caught,
In silly binds life has brought!

Guardians of Legacy

Oh the clan of stretchy loops,
Guardians of our goofy troops.
With colors brash, and charm so loud,
They wear their pride, so very proud.

In mismatched pairs our tale unfolds,
With lots of laughter, joy it holds.
Retelling moments, silly and sweet,
In a tangle where our hearts meet.

Each snap counts, a memory claimed,
No one's ever left unnamed.
Stampede of giggles, quite the sight,
These playful ties hold dreams so bright.

In humble threads, legends weave,
Silly slaps that we believe.
Dancing as the night draws near,
With every flick, we spread some cheer!

Reflections in the Dark

In the gloom, a flicker shines,
Laughter hides amid the lines.
Witty whispers float and sway,
As shadows tease and come to play.

Silly faces, echoes dart,
In this dance, we play our part.
Twirling 'round with silly grace,
Reflecting joy on every face.

Jokes and jests, a clever jest,
Hiding truths that make us blessed.
In the dark, we find our spark,
These goofy ties create the arc.

With every chuckle, mystery grows,
Blurs of laughter, who really knows?
Frolicking through the night so stark,
In playful banter, we leave our mark!

Bonds of Solidarity

Tangled yet, together stand,
A quirky troop, a shiny band.
With every yank and every twist,
Not a chance we'll be dismissed.

Side by side in ridiculous poses,
Amidst the chaos, laughter dozes.
Holding tight through every prank,
Unified, we form a rank.

Joyful jumps and silly screams,
Chasing folks in wacky dreams.
With every tug we share a deed,
In bonds of laughter, we all lead.

Connections made with playful flair,
Woven deep, beyond compare.
In this union, funny and free,
A spirited dance, just you and me!